INTRODUCTION

T he Yorkshire Dales have a character all their own – not just because of the diverse scenery but also because of the people who live there. The landscape has many contrasting elements – open fells, a few individual peaks and many valleys, while beneath the surface lies a vast network of caverns and connecting passageways, some of which still remain unexplored. Water cuts its way down fell sides to form gills, becks and falls, and frequently it disappears underground to reappear somewhere completely different. This limestone landscape is known as karst and has quite different characteristics from that formed on any other rock.

Above: Rise Hill, Dentdale

The Dales contain a unique and varied vegetation. In the limestone areas where the soil is thin and alkaline, there are rich, sweet pastures with a sub-Alpine flora including rare orchids, violets, cowslips, saxifrages and the delightful little bird's eye primrose. On the gritstone moorlands the soil is more acidic and sphagnum bog, peat-hags and cotton grass tend to dominate the scenery. In the east there is more heath and heather moorland.

Down in the valley bottoms the soil is more fertile, and here the land is settled and farmed. The hill farmers have been a part of the Dales life for centuries and, over many years, they have influenced the scenery that is so treasured today. The barns, the stone walls, and stolidly built farmhouses play their part in making up the familiar pattern of the Dales landscape.

Above: East Gill Foss, Swaledale

The remoteness of the individual valleys may be a factor in forming the distinctive character of Dalesfolk. Their relative isolation has tended to make them wary of outsiders and yet, once known, they become friends for life. Dales people are independent and resourceful but at the same time they form a close-knit, loyal and mutually supportive society.

It is these different aspects of the Yorkshire Dales that we have brought together in this booklet. The unexpected scenery, the caves, the unique flora and the Dalesfolk, help to make this area one of Britain's most precious heritages. With increased understanding it is hoped that these varying factors can be protected and conserved for future generations to enjoy.

Above: Bird's-Eye Primrose

THE DALES

There are many valleys that make up the Yorkshire Dales, from the largest, Wharfedale and Wensleydale, to the smallest, such as the remoter valleys of Walden Dale and Cotterdale. Although the many dales have certain features in common, each has its own separate identity. Some are wilder and more open, while others feel sheltered and enclosed. Limestone outcrops can give a rugged look to some, while others have a gentler landscape with a greater number of trees – birch, pine and hazel, reminding us of a time when, long ago, this part of Britain was thickly wooded.

Above: Wharfedale, with Kettlewell in the foreground

The Rivers Ure and Wharfe start out in narrow gills, but quickly develop into larger rivers creating the mature flat-bottomed valleys of Wensleydale and Wharfedale with their fertile meadowland. By contrast Dentdale and Swaledale rarely exceed half a mile in width, giving both the definitive scooped-out shape closely associated with most of the Yorkshire Dales.

Different again are the western dales of Chapel-le-Dale and Kingsdale; these are fine examples of U-shaped glacial valleys carved into an extensive limestone plateau. The retreat of the glaciers left prominent scars on either side of these dales giving them a bleaker, more barren appearance.

Above: Swaledale and the village of Muker

The Dales were settled by successive waves of people in a long, slow process extending over thousands of years. The Angles penetrated the Dales peacefully during the ninth and tenth centuries and settled in small, organized communities creating the villages we see today. They were arable farmers and preferred the land in the valley bottoms. By contrast the Norsemen came from the west and were great sheep farmers. They preferred to make clearings on the fellsides, leaving plenty of space between each farmstead for a substantial sheep-run. Evidence for this can be seen along the western dales of Dentdale and Garsdale.

Above left: Dentdale
Above right: The River Skirfare, Littondale

THE FELLS

The vast expanses of fell land that separate one dale from the next give the Yorkshire Dales their sense of wilderness. There are tracts of land where mile upon mile can be covered without meeting another soul. Out on the tops it feels open, unenclosed and free. The moorlands occupy the greater part of the land above a thousand feet, and are characterised by infertile, acid soils that support heathers, sedges and mountain grasses.

Above left: The fells above Wharfedale
Above right: Ingleborough from the summit of Whernside

By contrast with the steep-sided, well-defined peaks of the Lake District, the fells in the Yorkshire Dales have a rounder, gentler appearance. Here the hills seem to merge into the surrounding moorland and there appears little separation between land and sky. Although the fell can feel solitary it is never silent: against the noise of the wind and the bleating sheep, three distinctive bird songs haunt the fells in summer, the 'go-back, go-back' of the grouse, the cry of the curlew, and the single, melancholy note of the golden plover.

Above: The Buttertubs Pass, looking towards Swaledale

Of the few obvious peaks, the best known are Pen-y-ghent, Ingleborough, Whernside and Wild Boar Fell. The summit cliffs of these hills give them more clearly defined aspects. In the past the fell tops provided settlement sites for early man. For example, Ingleborough, with its distinctive flat top of millstone grit, appears to have been used as a defensive fort and refuge by the Brigantes against the Romans. Now, the familiarly shaped peak serves as a reference point for walkers, and can be seen from as far away as the southern fells of the Lake District.

Above: Whernside from the slopes of Ingleborough

THE GEOLOGY OF THE DALES

The Dales landscape owes its appearance to erosion by glacial action and the processes of weathering on the underlying rock. Most of this rock is made up of solidified sediment, laid down in horizontal layers under a tropical sea about 300 million years ago. Violent earth movements then raised up these

Above: Gordale Scar

rocks in successive stages, fracturing them into a network of cracks and fissures. In some areas the fissures allowed hot fluids carrying lead and other minerals to flow up through them, creating the ore-fields of Swaledale and other sites.

The most striking of these sedimentary rocks is the two-hundred-metre-thick Great Scar Limestone, which gives rise to the karst landscape for which the Dales are famous. Overlaying this is the Yoredale series, which consists of a succession of thinly bedded limestones, sandstones and shales. And topping all these is the Millstone Grit, which forms the summit rock of most of the higher peaks.

Above: The glaciated limestone scars of Chapel-le-Dale

During and after the Ice Ages the shape of the Dales was radically modified. The grinding action of the ice and the abrasive power of the melt water helped deepen and widen the valleys, scouring the surface rock and leaving behind numerous small crags or 'scars'. Great stretches of bare limestone were also left exposed. These were subsequently attacked by rainwater, which seeped into the cracks and fissures, opening them up into 'grykes', and leaving behind 'clints', or blocks of rock in between. Fine examples of this limestone pavement can be seen on the flanks of Ingleborough and above Malham cove.

Above left: Fossil crinoids in limestone
Above centre: Limestone pavement below Ingleborough
Above right: Wood anemones in Gryke

THE CAVES

lthough the limestone scars, pavements, and gorges are the most obvious features of karst scenery, in addition to these there is the hidden world of caves. As rain water continues to dissolve the limestone, it percolates deeper underground, leaving dry valleys on the surface and opening up caves beneath. The Yorkshire Dales contain Britain's most important series of caves, which range in size from holes a few metres long to the sixty or more kilometres of the Easegill System. Although cave exploration has a surprisingly long history, and several of the Dales caves have been known for hundreds of years, caving only

Above: Stream Passage, Lost John's Cave

started seriously here around the middle of the 19th century.

The early pioneers carried out some remarkable feats of exploration, considering their heavy, cumbersome equipment and primitive lighting. Nowadays, with modern clothing, efficient lamps, and sophisticated rope techniques, caving is easier and more pleasant, yet still not without its excitement or dangers. The attractions of the underground world can tempt the inexperienced into visiting caves inadequately equipped, and without understanding that caves flood very quickly and severely.

But the lure of caving is understandable. Over thousands of years, a myriad of passage-ways in a bewildering array of shapes and sizes has been created.

Above left: Rowten Pot's 220ft shaft
Above right: Straw stalactites in Hagg Gill Pot

In some of the caves spectacular, vertical shafts of hundreds of feet lead to hidden grottoes, beautifully decorated with stalactites and stalagmites. In others, there are huge chambers such as that at the bottom of Gaping Gill. These are the hidden treasures of the Yorkshire Dales.

Above: The Main Chamber of Gaping Gill

DALES WEATHER

I t is the unpredictability of Dales weather that not only surprises the visitor, but also makes life very difficult for the farmer. There seems to be no logical sequence to the weather patterns. New Year's Day can be like the first day of spring and in April a farmer can be digging out snow-bound sheep. The weather also changes drastically as height is gained. A gentle breeze down dale can become a ferocious gale on the fell, and a thin drizzle in the village can concentrate itself higher up to become thick mist, making disorientation easy for the walker.

Above: Storm clouds over Wensleydale

As an upland area in the path of Atlantic depressions, inevitably the Yorkshire Dales get their share of wet weather. However, when the rain comes, there are compensations. Waterfalls and becks abound in the Dales and they can easily fill to capacity, creating surging torrents that tumble down the fell sides and feed the bigger rivers to bursting point. A 'waterfalls' walk on a wet day can be a spectacle in itself, but care should always be taken. Whereas in normal weather conditions it is harmless fun to walk behind Hardraw Force, this is certainly not the case after a downpour! And for many years there have been casualties at the Ingleton Waterfalls.

Above left: Hardraw Force
Above right: Thornton Force in flood

In a bad year the fell roads can remain blocked for much of the winter, but the snow ploughs and gritters work hard to keep the lower roads open all the year round. Blizzard conditions, white-outs, hail and bitter winds are easily capable of overcoming the most intrepid walker out on the fell. No true Dalesman remains unprepared for the speed with which weather can change in the hills.

Above: Whatever the weather, there is work to be done

The weather tends to come in cycles. Either depressions can blow in for weeks on end and it seems the sun never shines, or, alternatively, hot fine weather may persist throughout the summer months. When this is the case, the Dales can boast of being one of the most beautiful parts of Europe.

Above: Morning mist over Dentdale

THE FARMING YEAR

T he main occupation among Dales people is farming, just as it has been for many centuries. There is little else that the fells can be used for apart from rearing hardy sheep. The farming year begins around October, when the tups are brought in to be put to the ewes. Each good tup will have as many as sixty or more ewes to run with, so the farmer has to make sure that his tups are well fed and fit for the job! Ruddle is painted on the tup's underside so that when it mounts the ewe a bright patch of colour will appear on her back, acting as a guide as to when she will lamb. In the middle of December the ewes are returned to the fell to cope with the winter as best they may.

Above left: Tupping time at Malham
Above right: The ewes are brought in to meet the tups

During the colder months the shepherd will watch the weather and, when possible, bring the sheep further down the fell if bad snow is forecast. If sheep are out on the high fell in a bad snowstorm, they will seek shelter behind walls and in dips and hollows, and it is in such places that they are most likely to get buried by drifting snow. Nowadays the ewes are fed regularly from January to lambing-time, and this allows a chance for the farmer to check that they are keeping well. The ewes winter better with extra hay and feed-nuts, and this also helps ensure that their lambs are healthier and there is plenty of ewe milk.

Above: Looking for buried sheep after a snowstorm in Deepdale

April is the busiest month of the year. A conscientious shepherd will try to get round his flock four or five times a day, keeping a watch out for any problems. There can be malpresentations, shearlings that are lambing for the first time, lambs that are too big for the ewe, numerous infections that can spread, and lambs that simply refuse to suck – a whole catalogue of possible disasters. But nurturing this year's lamb crop is taking care of the annual income: a lamb or ewe that is lost is a financial loss, so no shepherd can afford to cut corners.

Above: Marking lambs – families work together on the hill farms

June is a quieter month – a time for spring-cleaning the barns of winter muck and preparing for the summer tasks of clipping and haytime. The problem with both these tasks is that they depend upon fine weather. Fleeces cannot be stored damp or they will rot, and hay needs three sunny days in which the cut grass can be turned before it is baled up. It is no wonder that more and more farmers are making silage instead; for silage the grass can be cut, rolled and bagged while it is still damp.

Although farming ways will inevitably change over the years, the affection that the Dalesfolk have for their sheep and for the fells has not altered since the time when the Norsemen made clearings for their sheep-runs in the tenth century.

Above: Haytime

THE DALES PEOPLE

Although farming has always been the main occupation in the Yorkshire Dales, many other and varying influences have left their mark upon the area. Whether it was the Normans who imposed their authority by building castles, or the great monastic houses bequeathing their famous abbeys, or the Victorians' engineering feats such as the building of the Settle to Carlisle Railway, each generation has succeeded in stamping its mark upon the land.

Above left: Pendragon Castle in the Eden Valley
Above right: Jervaulx Abbey
Lower left: The Lofthouse and Middlesmoor Silver Band plays at the Tan Hill Sheep Show
Lower right: Gala day – knocking each other off the horse!

Industries have come and gone with the times. Mining flourished until the late nineteenth century, because improved mechanization allowed deeper shafts to be sunk, and power could be provided to service both the mines and smelt mills. This was a time when the Dales mines succeeded in producing most of the country's lead. Smaller cottage industries, such as home knitting, had a strong tradition in the northern dales, but this dwindled at the turn of the twentieth century. Knitting sticks are now museum pieces, and mining remains stand only as monuments to the Dales' industrial past.

Above: "Lord Nelson" on Artengill Viaduct – Settle to Carlisle Railway

Nowadays quarrying is the only industry on any sizeable scale. The Dales quarries are controlled by multi-national corporations and produce substantial amounts of high quality limestone which is used in the steel industry and for the building of roads. Although valued as a source of local employment, the quarries leave behind hideous scars on the landscape to the regret of many.

Smaller businesses are more in tune with the Dales way of life. There is always plenty of work for builders and joiners who take pride in using traditional methods and materials in pursuit of their craft. And products made by local artists, such as hand-knitted sweaters, jewellery, paintings and wooden ornaments, now have

Above: Dent Village

outlets in the art and craft shops that can be found in most dales. In recent years there has been a steady flow of incomers to the Dales, some to seek work and others to retire. A blend of different people from varied backgrounds now makes up the Dales population and, no doubt, many of those will also leave their mark on Dales life in years to come.

Above left: Cabinet maker Colin Gardner carves a Yorkshire rose on a specially designed seat that converts into a 'welly box'!
Above right: Mrs Mary Guy knits cardigans for Swaledale Woollens using local wool
Lower left: Hubberholme Church in Wharfedale
Lower right: The remains of a lead-mining hamlet in Arkengarthdale are now used as a sheep pen

CONSERVATION

I t is not just the landscape of the Yorkshire Dales that needs protecting and caring for, but its traditions and culture as well. Although buildings, stone walls, flora and fauna require conservation measures, it is the livelihoods of the farmers that need supporting too. For centuries the Dalesfolk have worked the land and we should not forget that they are its true custodians.

Above: Traditional hay meadow in Swaledale

In this technological age, farmers need encouragement to care for the land sensitively, otherwise there is a danger that pressures of the market place can overcome other considerations. However, some schemes are now being put forward that are designed to redress the balance. For example, in certain areas farmers are being given financial incentives to revert to traditional methods of haymaking, so that the meadows can once again abound in wild flowers. It is to be hoped that more such ideas will follow.

Above left: Wood Cranesbill
Above centre: Small White Orchid
Above right: Water Avens

Nature Reserves have been set up to protect some of the rarer species of flowers. On some areas of the limestone pavement Angular Solomon's Seal, Baneberry, Globe Flower, Lily of the Valley, and several cranesbills, are able to thrive in their natural environment.

Unfortunately the visitors who love to visit the Dales can also cause damage. Footpath erosion is a major concern on many of the more popular fells. But some of

Above left: Angular Solomon's Seal
Above right: Globe Flowers in Colt Park Wood with Pen-y-ghent
in the background

the most beautiful parts of the Yorkshire Dales are off the beaten track, and the spirit of the fells is most keenly felt where there is a greater chance of solitude. There is no reason for the more obvious walks to be tramped to destruction when there are so many fells and dales where walkers can roam with freedom.

Above: The Yorkshire Dales National Park has used duck-boarding to help combat the problem of footpath erosion.

N owadays more and more people are enjoying
the Dales at different times of year, easing the
pressure of tourism during those summer
months. Winter walking can be stimulating and
rewarding, especially when there is a sharp frost or a
smattering of snow on the ground. It is then that the
Yorkshire Dales take on a rare, stark beauty, helping to
remind us how important it is to preserve these last wild
areas of England.

Above: Dent Keld